TABLE OF CONTENTS

Novel-Ties® are printed on recycled paper.

Copyright © 2005, 2012 by LEARNING LINKS

For the Teacher

This reproducible study guide to use in conjunction with *Chasing Vermeer* consists of lessons for guided reading. Written in chapter-by-chapter format, the guide contains a synopsis, pre-reading activities, vocabulary and comprehension exercises, as well as extension activities to be used as follow-up to the novel.

In a homogeneous classroom, whole class instruction with one title is appropriate. In a heterogeneous classroom, reading groups should be formed: each group works on a different novel at its reading level. Depending upon the length of time devoted to reading in the classroom, each novel, with its guide and accompanying lessons, may be completed in three to six weeks.

Begin using NOVEL-TIES for reading development by distributing the novel and a folder to each child. Distribute duplicated pages of the study guide for students to place in their folders. After examining the cover and glancing through the book, students can participate in several pre-reading activities. Vocabulary questions should be considered prior to reading a chapter; all other work should be done after the chapter has been read. Comprehension questions can be answered orally or in writing. The classroom teacher should determine the amount of work to be assigned, always keeping in mind that readers must be nurtured and that the ultimate goal is encouraging students' love of reading.

The benefits of using NOVEL-TIES are numerous. Students read good literature in the original, rather than in abridged or edited form. The good reading habits, formed by practice in focusing on interpretive comprehension and literary techniques, will be transferred to the books students read independently. Passive readers become active, avid readers.

SYNOPSIS

One October evening, three Chicago residents received a copy of the same troubling, anonymous letter. In these letters, the writer stated that he believed a crime involving a great artist from the past had been committed—a crime that dated back many centuries. He wanted the letters to be kept secret until a famous painting by the Dutch artist Jan Vermeer would be stolen. Along with the rest of the country, the sixth-graders in Ms. Hussey's class at the Chicago Laboratory School got caught up in an important debate over who really painted some of the pictures attributed to Vermeer. But who was the art scholar who wrote the three letters and presumably stole the painting? And what would happen if the letter-writer's demands to museum and government authorities were not met?

Petra Andalee and Calder Pillay were neighbors and classmates who had a keen interest in solving this mystery. With the help of a set of pentominoes (pattern pieces used by mathematicians) and their own powers of observation, Petra and Calder pursued the case. Calder looked for patterns while Petra received supernatural messages from a woman in an old painting—the very painting that was stolen as it was on its way to a Chicago museum.

Petra and Calder noticed that there were clues and patterns all around, but they could not discern their meaning. They wondered whether Ms. Hussey, their teacher, was a suspect? They suspected that Mr. Watch, the bookshop owner, and Mrs. Sharpe, a widow whose husband had died in pursuit of information about a Vermeer painting, were involved in the theft. Even Petra's and Calder's parents seemed to be hiding an involvement. When Calder received upsetting news about an old friend and a child who may have been kidnapped, it seemed that everything in his familiar world had been turned upside down.

The art thief informed the press that the stolen painting would be destroyed if his demands were not met. Petra and Calder increased their efforts to find the precious picture, feeling sure that it was somewhere nearby. Their search led them into danger when they finally located the picture, hidden in one of the University buildings. In a suspenseful chase scene, Petra rescued the painting, while Calder was assaulted by the thief.

At the conclusion of the story, the painting was restored to the authorities and the connections among the strange events of that autumn were revealed. For the students in Ms. Hussey's class, school would never again be dull because they had learned to appreciate history and art, and to question old assumptions and ideas. Petra and Calder had come to understand that to solve a problem a person just had to know how to ask the right questions.

BACKGROUND INFORMATION

Baroque Art in the Netherlands

During the seventeenth century, the Netherlands was divided along political and religious lines. This was the period of the Counter-Reformation, during which the Roman Catholic Church attempted to suppress the Protestant faith that was gaining strength in Europe. In the northern provinces of Holland, people battled for independence while in the Catholic south, Spanish rule prevailed.

The seventeenth century was an age of lavish display known as the Baroque period. Nobles, prosperous merchants, and church leaders hired artists and architects to build and decorate elaborate churches, palaces, and homes. At the same time, middle class people supported a market for paintings and prints on a smaller scale.

The painters of the Dutch and Flemish schools, such as Peter Paul Rubens, Rembrandt, Anthony van Dyck, and Johannes (Jan) Vermeer, worked in varying modes. Their subjects ranged from the Bible and ancient mythology to the homey business of daily life. These and many other painters transformed interior scenes, still-lifes, and portraiture into high art. Many paintings of the period were rich in pattern and detail, causing some people to believe that the works contained hidden messages and themes.

Jan Vermeer and the Delft School

The "Delft School," named after a city in the southwest Netherlands, blended the objective Dutch style of representational painting with a more romantic Italian influence. This group of artists, which included such masters as Carel Fabritius, Pieter de Hooch, Houckgeest, van Vliet, and Jan Vermeer, explored color and optics, the study of light. Vermeer is known to have experimented with the *camera obscura*, a device which could accurately project images of sunlit objects. In another advance, the Delft painters began using linseed oil from Flanders to blend their dried pigments. The resulting oil-based paint made it possible to work more delicately with line and contour.

Jan Vermeer (1632–1665), whose small output and relatively brief life probably account for his lack of popularity during his own time, is regarded today as one of the great artists of Europe. Very little is known about his life. The son of a silk worker with an interest in the art trade, Vermeer followed in his father's footsteps, but soon became a painter in his own right. His first work of art is dated 1656. Vermeer belonged to a local artists' guild and may have studied with either Leonaert Bramer or Carel Fabritius, two notable painters of Delft. In 1654, Vermeer married Catharina Bolnes. The couple had eleven children to raise, a circumstance undoubtedly connected to the painter's decline into poverty. Vermeer spent his entire life in Delft. For over two centuries after his death, his work was disregarded or attributed to other Dutch artists. It was not until the mid-nineteenth century that the French art critic W. Thore-Burger brought Vermeer's paintings to the attention of the public.

Background Information (cont.)

Art experts now regard Vermeer as the greatest of the Dutch colorists. He was meticulous in his preparation of paints and experimented with different formulas in order to create a variety of textures on canvas. He tended to prefer vibrant yellows and blues. Working sometimes with thick, rich color, at other times with thin glazes that allowed greater transparency, Vermeer created thirty-five paintings, a small but stunning collection. He is best known for interior scenes and portraits; in many of his paintings, the figures of one or two women dominate a scene. The human figures are typically engaged in some ordinary activity, which Vermeer manages to transform into something both graceful and profound. In his later works, color effects are achieved by attention to the way that light from a window plays on objects in a room.

Today we can study Vermeer's techniques with the help of any of a number of written and on-line guides to his work. His paintings are displayed in some of the world's great art museums, in reproductions, and on the Internet where several websites are devoted to his art.

PRE-READING ACTIVITIES AND DISCUSSION QUESTIONS

1. Preview the book by reading the title and author's name and by looking at the illustration on the cover. What do you think the book will be about? When and where do you think it takes place?

2. Read the Background Information on page two of this study guide. Do some additional research to learn more about Vermeer and the other artists who formed the Delft School of painting. Start a **K-W-L** chart, such as the one below. Fill in the first two columns before you read the book. Fill in column three after you finish the book.

Vermeer and the Delft School		
– K – **What I Know**	**– W –** **What I Want To Know**	**– L –** **What I Learned**

3. Read the maxim written by Charles Fort, at the beginning of the book. What do you think it means? How might learning make someone uncomfortable? How might it be good to be uncomfortable?

4. Look carefully at the Chasing Vermeer Map Key at the beginning of the novel. In what direction would you need to walk going from Calder's to Petra's house? How many blocks away from Calder's house is Fargo Hall? How many blocks would Petra have to walk to get to Delia Dell Hall? Refer to this map as you read the book.

5. Read about pentominoes and the *Challenge to the Reader* at the beginning of the novel. See if you can decode the hidden message formed by the illustrations. Also, notice the little animal that appears in many of the pictures. Compare your conclusions with those of your classmates.

6. The main characters in this novel try to solve a mystery using certain clues. With a partner, discuss how everyday life can contain puzzles or mysteries begging to be solved. Present an oral report about a mysterious situation that you attempted to explain, and what you finally discovered.

7. **Art Connection:** Experts study works of art to discover who created them or from which period of history they originated. Choose a painting or sculpture from long ago and do some research to find out about its origins. Write a report about the work of art and the person who created it, including any historical details that provide a context for the artwork.

8. In this novel, several characters are not who they seem to be. What other works of fiction have you read in which a character's identity or motivation provides the source of confusion or mystery? Make a list of these stories, books, or plays.

9. **Art Connection:** Go online or look at art magazines to find photos or illustrations of paintings by Jan Vermeer. Display these in your classroom as you read this book, and observe the details that compose each work of art, such as the objects in the background, the garments worn by the subjects, and the expression shown on the model's face.

CHAPTERS 1 – 4

Vocabulary: Antonyms are words with opposite meanings. Draw a line from each word in Column A to its antonym in Column B. Then use the words in Column A to complete the sentences below.

1. amply
2. flattered
3. pretentious
4. agitated
5. gullible
6. brutal
7. determined
8. artificial

a. calm
b. gentle
c. insufficiently
d. wavering
e. insulted
f. natural
g. modest
h. suspicious

. . . .

1. The _____ young man was soon cheated out of his money by the clever con man.

2. Everyone was fooled into thinking that the _____ silk roses were real.

3. When attacked, an ordinarily gentle person may react in a(n) _____ way.

4. Once they had rested and been _____ fed, the hikers continued on their way.

5. Everyone in the building became _____ when the alarm sounded.

6. The artist was _____ to receive an excellent review from an important art critic.

7. The _____ salesman rang doorbells up and down the block until he found a customer for his set of encyclopedias.

8. I didn't want my home to be so _____ that my friends would feel uncomfortable visiting me.

> Read to find out how Ms. Hussey got Petra and Calder to think about art.

Chapters 1 – 4 (cont.)

Questions:

1. Why did three people living alone in Chicago have trouble sleeping on a warm October night?

2. Why were Calder and the other students fascinated by Ms. Hussey and the way she conducted her class?

3. How did Calder relate his pentomino pieces to Ms. Hussey's first assignment?

4. Why was Petra upset by her encounters with Calder and Ms. Hussey at Powell's Used Books?

5. Why was Petra unhappy at home?

6. Why did the author describe both Petra and Calder as "hybrid" kids?

7. Why did Ms. Hussey take her class on a field trip to the Art Institute of Chicago?

Questions for Discussion:

1. Why do you think each of the three people received the letter?

2. Do you agree with Petra that "humans needed questions more than answers?"

3. Would you like to be a student in Ms. Hussey's class?

4. Why do you think Petra's mother and father argued about a letter and then destroyed it?

5. How do you think the mysterious letter and Ms. Hussey's assignment to find a life-changing letter might be connected?

6. How do you interpret the artist Picasso's statement, "Art is a lie, but a lie that tells the truth?" How would you paraphrase this statement?

7. What do you think the short excerpt from *Lo!* is all about? Why do you think frogs are mentioned so often?

Literary Devices:

I. *Metaphor*—A metaphor is a suggested or implied comparison between two unlike objects. For example:

Petra's household was a tornado where life swirled in noisy circles.

What is being compared?

_____

Why is this an apt comparison?

_____

_____

Chapters 1 – 4 (cont.)

II. *Personification*—Personification is a figure of speech in which an author grants human characteristics to nonhuman objects. For example:

> This year a trumpet vine leaned eagerly against a cool lily, pointy leaves fought to see who could take over the steps, purples and blood reds argued loudly with each other.

What is being personified?

_____

Rewrite this sentence in your own words and compare your rewrite to the original. What is gained or lost by your paraphrase?

_____

_____

Literary Element: Characterization

Use the Venn diagram below to begin a comparison of the characters of Petra and Calder. Record their similarities in the overlapping part of the circles. Add information as you continue to read the book.

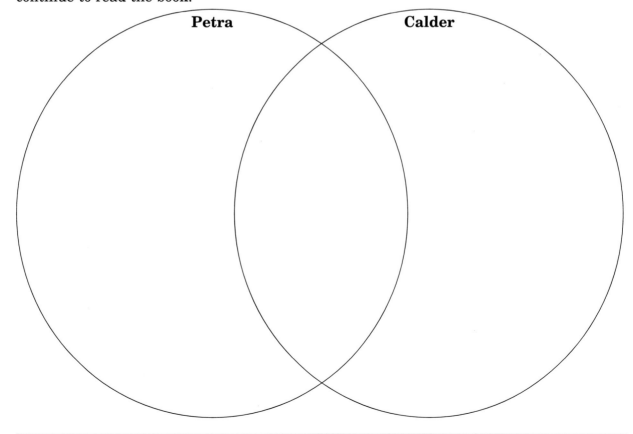

Chapters 1 – 4 (cont.)

Art Connections:

1. Find reproductions of the work of the late French Impressionist artist Gustave Caillebotte. Focus on the *Rainy Day* painting that Petra enjoyed or choose another painting in his body of work. Decide whether there is anything fascinating, interesting, or mysterious to you about the work.

2. Work with a small group of your classmates to arrive at a definition of art. What makes something a work of art? Compare your responses with those of your classmates.

Math Connection:

Study the pentominoes shown in the book, and make your own set out of cardboard or oaktag. Experiment with the pieces and see what kinds of puzzle shapes you can make with them.

Social Studies Connections:

1. Do some research to find out about the educator John Dewey. How did his work and theories help to shape modern-day education? Prepare a brief oral report about Dewey's significant contributions.

2. Read about the ancient stone city of Petra in Jordan. Find pictures that show the restored city today.

Writing Activities:

1. Write a letter to a friend or family member in which you try to convince him or her to believe or act in a particular way. Make your letter as persuasive as possible.

2. Write about an unusual person who has influenced you or helped to shape your ideas.

CHAPTERS 5 – 8

Vocabulary: Synonyms are words with similar meanings. Draw a line from each word in Column A to its synonym in Column B. Then use the words in Column A to fill in the blanks in the sentences below.

<u>A</u>	<u>B</u>
1. bizarre	a. confused
2. venomous	b. average
3. disoriented	c. strange
4. profound	d. poisonous
5. exhilarating	e. copy
6. mediocre	f. deep
7. inexplicable	g. thrilling
8. reproduction	h. unexplainable

· ·

1. Although the language of the poem was simple, it had a(n) _____ effect on every part of our lives.

2. Only a detective could have made sense of the seemingly _____ clues collected at the scene of the crime.

3. The value of the painting fell as soon as it became clear that it was a(n) _____.

4. In her Halloween costume of huge gray wig, pointy shoes, and old-fashioned gown, my five-year-old sister had a distinctly _____ appearance.

5. The first snowfall of the year was so _____ that we all ran outdoors to make snowmen and go sledding.

6. It is important to seek immediate medical help if you are bitten by a(n) _____ snake.

7. The accident victim, unable to remember his name and address, was obviously _____ by the experience.

8. Having spent little time preparing my book report, I expected a(n) _____ grade.

> Read to find out how the seventeenth century artist Jan Vermeer came into the lives of Calder and Petra.

Chapters 5 – 8 (cont.)

Questions:

1. Why was Petra fascinated with *Lo!*, a strange book written by Charles Fort?

2. What did Charles Fort mean when he wrote, "We fit standards to judgments"?

3. What did Petra learn from her vision of the old-fashioned woman who appeared to her in a half-dream?

4. Why did Calder choose the picture on his cherished wooden box to fulfill Ms. Hussey's art assignment?

5. Why were both Calder and Petra interested in Mrs. Sharpe?

6. Why did Mrs. Sharpe invite Calder and Petra to tea?

7. Why was Calder amazed by the painting that hung on Mrs. Sharpe's wall?

8. Why was Calder fascinated with the life and work of the artist Jan Vermeer?

9. Why was Petra shocked to see a copy of the painting "A Lady Writing" in Calder's book of Vermeer paintings?

Questions for Discussion:

1. Have you ever been in a situation where you or people you know inadvertently twisted what was actually observed to fit what they believed should have been there?

2. Why do you think Petra was fascinated by the sentence in *Lo!* that stated, "We shall pick up an existence by its frogs"? What do you think Charles Fort meant?

3. Do you think Calder gave his friend Tommy good advice in the coded message?

4. What relationship might there be among the unusual circumstances recorded by Charles Fort and the missing boy in Tommy's coded message and Mrs. Sharpe?

5. Why do you suppose it was in Calder's yard that Petra found a copy of the mysterious letter? Who do you think discarded the letter, and why?

6. If you were to experience a series of coincidences would you attribute it to chance, the supernatural, or would you search for some other cause?

Math Connections:

1. Choose a room in your house or at school and notice the geometry of shapes, shadows, and reflections all around you. What shapes and patterns do you see?

2. Study the pentomino code on page 57 and decode the message Tommy wrote to Calder. Write the full message on paper and compare your response with that of a classmate.

Chapters 5 – 8 (cont.)

Literary Devices:

I. *Cliffhanger*—A cliffhanger is a device borrowed from serialized silent film in which an episode ends at a moment of suspense. In a novel, it usually appears at the end of a chapter to encourage the reader to continue on in the book. What is the cliffhanger at the end of Chapter Five?

_____

_____

II. Simile—A simile is a figure of speech in which two unlike objects are compared using the words "like" or "as." For example:

> This was a calm, deliberate world, a world where dreams were real and each syllable held the light like a pearl.

What is being compared?

_____

What does this reveal about the significance of the written word?

_____

_____

_____

Writing Activities:

1. Choose an object that you consider a work of art and write a description of it, including details about its appearance and the style in which it is executed. Use Petra or Calder's writing for the art assignment as a model.

2. Write a journal entry about a vivid dream you can recall clearly. Why was this dream meaningful to you? What do you think the people, objects, and actions in the dream represent?

3. Work with a partner to conduct a coded correspondence, such as the correspondence Calder carried on with Tommy. Base your correspondence on the pentomino code on page fifty-seven. Write about a real or imagined mysterious circumstance.

CHAPTERS 9 – 12

Vocabulary: Draw a line from each word on the left to its definition on the right. Then use the numbered words to fill in the blanks in the sentences below.

	A		B
1.	incalculable	a.	being done without any delay
2.	ingenious	b.	quality of being hidden or unclear
3.	attribute	c.	uncertain or unpredictable
4.	obscurity	d.	original and clever
5.	intimidated	e.	lacking in strength or vitality
6.	instantaneous	f.	wise; discreet
7.	judicious	g.	threatened; made fearful
8.	subdued	h.	reckon as belonging to; ascribe

· ·

1. Only after careful examination could the art critics _____ a newly discovered piece of sculpture to the famous artist Michelangelo.

2. The mail carrier was so _____ by the growling guard dogs that she refused to leave mail at the house.

3. Once a star of Hollywood films, the elderly actress had faded into _____.

4. Her reaction to the news was _____, immediately leaping up and beginning to clap her hands and cheer.

5. Known for always making _____ decisions, John was approached by friends who had problems.

6. The children, usually bright and lively, seemed _____ when their parents told them the family was moving to another city.

7. At the beginning of the twentieth century, the automobile seemed like a(n) _____ invention to those who only knew horse-drawn carriages.

8. Despite advanced telescopes, there is still a(n) _____ number of stars in our galaxy.

> Read to find out what happened to *A Lady Writing*.

Chapters 9 – 12 (cont.)

Questions:

1. Why did Calder and Petra begin to do research on Vermeer's life?

2. Why did Calder and Petra telephone the National Gallery of Art?

3. Why did Calder worry about his father?

4. Why were Petra and Calder particularly upset about the theft of the Vermeer painting, *A Lady Writing*?

5. Why were Calder and Petra worried about Ms. Hussey?

6. Why was the *The Lady Writing* stolen?

7. How did the Vermeer case help to teach Ms. Hussey's students about art scholarship?

8. Why was Calder amazed as soon as he entered Mrs. Sharpe's kitchen?

9. How did Mrs. Sharpe respond to Petra's and Calder's questions? Why did her reaction make them think she might be involved in the art theft?

Questions for Discussion:

1. Do you agree with Petra that we are surrounded by coincidences and overlapping ideas, but that we fail to notice them?

2. Do you think that any set of circumstances could justify the theft of a painting?

3. Do you think that Petra and Calder should have told Ms. Hussey what they knew about the Vermeer case?

4. Why do you think Mrs. Sharpe invited Calder and Petra to tea? Why did she dismiss them so abruptly?

Literary Device: Foreshadowing

Foreshadowing refers to the clues or hints an author provides to suggest what will happen later in the novel. What might Ms. Hussey's accident foreshadow?

_____

_____

Chapters 9 – 12 (cont.)

Literary Element: Plot

Plot refers to the sequence of events in a work of fiction. To keep track of the plot in this complicated book, list in the chart below, all of the mysteries you have encountered so far. Then record how each of these mysteries is resolved.

Mystery	Resolution

Chapters 9 – 12 (cont.)

Math Connection:

Use your knowledge of the secret code on page fifty-seven to decipher the new message from Tommy.

Art Connection:

Do some research to find out about each of Vermeer's paintings that have been stolen over the years. Prepare a report that shows where, when, and how the paintings were stolen, and whether or not they were later recovered.

Writing Activity:

Imagine that you are a concerned citizen with a strong interest in art. Write a letter for newspaper publication in which you respond to the "terrorist" letter, stating your own opinions and feelings about the theft.

CHAPTERS 13 – 16

Vocabulary: Use the context to choose the best definition for the underlined word in each of the following sentences. Circle the letter of the definition you choose.

1. No matter how hard we tried to erase the message, the page written in underline indelible ink had to be destroyed.

    a. can be easily erased   b. cannot be erased   c. transparent   d. black

2. If you are unwilling to reveal your identity, you must send an article anonymously.

    a. mysteriously   b. well-written   c. without a   d. without a
                                                             purpose   name

3. With donations of food and clothing, we showed that we were sympathetic to the problems of the flood victims.

    a. compassionate   b. indulgent   c. emotional   d. indifferent

4. We abandoned the picnic site as soon as we heard thunder in the distance.

    a. noticed   b. covered   c. deserted   d. approached

5. I felt queasy during the plane's choppy landing.

    a. excited   b. nauseated   c. odd   d. heroic

6. As soon as people entered the room, the mice scurried back into their holes.

    a. moved fast   b. walked slowly   c. squirmed   d. slid

7. It's hard to remain cheerful on a dismal, rainy day.

    a. damp   b. cheerful   c. dreary   d. sunny

8. My little brother glowered at me as I tried to take away his toy.

    a. charged   b. laughed   c. smiled   d. glared

> Read to find out how Petra and Calder tried to solve the mystery of the art theft.

Questions:

1. In what possible ways did Petra and Calder think Ms. Hussey might be implicated in the art theft?

2. Why did the authorities decide to ban the publication of further messages from the art bandit?

3. Why was Calder eager to deliver the books to Mrs. Sharpe?

Chapters 13 – 16 (cont.)

4. Why did Calder think that he had to rescue Tommy?

5. What did Calder's father recall about the late Mr. Sharpe? Why did the children doubt the accuracy of his remarks?

6. Why did Mrs. Sharpe request police protection?

7. Why was Ms. Hussey released from jail so quickly?

8. What conclusion did Petra and Calder jump to concerning Ms. Hussey and Mrs. Sharpe's connection to the art theft?

9. Why did Petra and Calder decide to search the University school premises for the missing canvas?

Questions for Discussion:

1. What would you do if you received a copy of the mysterious letter?

2. Do you suspect that any of the characters in the story are guilty of the art theft?

3. Why do you suppose Mrs. Sharpe chose that particular moment to reveal that she had received a letter from the "scholarly terrorist?"

4. How do you think the fate of Mrs. Sharpe's husband might have influenced her behavior in the Vermeer case?

5. What do you imagine Calder had actually found in the package stored in the basement of the school building?

Literary Element: Cliffhanger

What is the cliffhanger at the end of Chapter Sixteen?

Writing Activities:

1. Imagine you are Calder and Petra and write a journal entry describing your thoughts and feelings about the art theft. Also explain why you are interested in solving the crime.

2. Imagine that you are a student in Ms. Hussey's class, and write an editorial for your school newspaper expressing your opinion about how the case should be handled.

CHAPTERS 17 – 20

Vocabulary: Word analogies are equations in which the first pair of words has the same relationship as the second pair of words. For example: HURRY is to RUSH as SLEEP is to SLUMBER. Both pairs of words are synonyms. Choose the best word from the Word Box to complete each of the analogies below.

WORD BOX			
brusque	elegant	geologist	murky
courtyard	fraud	luminous	vigorously

1. SUCCESS is to EFFORT as _____ is to DISHONESTY.

2. WHEEL is to HUB as BUILDING is to _____.

3. RAPIDLY is to SLOWLY as GENTLY is to _____.

4. TASTEFUL is to _____ as SAD is to GLUM.

5. _____ is to CLEAR as ROUGH is to SMOOTH.

6. HURRICANE is to WINDY as MOON is to _____.

7. _____ is to BLUNT as CROOKED is to BENT.

8. ASTRONOMER is to STARS as _____ is to ROCKS.

Read to find out how Calder and Petra went about trying to find the stolen painting.

Questions:

1. In what ways did the Vermeer art theft have positive results?

2. Why was Mrs. Sharpe taken to the hospital?

3. How were Petra and Calder saved from "a life of crime"?

4. Why did Mrs. Sharpe forgive the children after Petra confessed that they had almost opened her letter?

5. How did Tommy add more mystery to the Vermeer art theft?

6. How did Mrs. Sharpe seem to give Petra and Calder clues to the whereabouts of the missing painting?

7. Why did Petra's father say that the scholarly terrorist was a "lunatic"? What had the thief threatened to do?

8. What had encouraged the art thief to believe that the demands would be met by art historians and museum curators?

Chapters 17 – 20 (cont.)

Questions for Discussion:

1. Do you think that the theft of the painting turned out to have more good or bad consequences?

2. Do you believe that the seemingly mysterious events were connected, or do you think they were simply coincidences?

3. How do you think Petra and Calder influenced one another's way of observing the world? Do you think these characters have changed since the beginning of the story?

Literary Devices:

I. *Analogy*—An analogy in literature refers to a comparison between two or more similar objects so as to suggest that if they are alike in some ways, they will probably be alike in other ways as well. For example, as Petra recalled how she felt as she walked down the staircase at Delia Dell Hall:

> There had been a clear *zap* in her mind. It reminded her of the time she'd been plugging a frayed lamp cord into the wall and her finger had landed on a bare wire.

What is being compared?

_____

_____

What do these two events have in common?

_____

_____

II. *Irony*—Irony refers to a twist of fate or a situation that turns out to be the opposite of what is expected. What is the irony attached to Frank's conversation with his daughter Petra?

_____

_____

_____

Chapters 17 – 20 (cont.)

III. *Point of view*—Point of view refers to the voice telling the story. It could be one of the characters or the author narrating. This story is told by the author as narrator. What problems would ensue if the author tried to tell this same story from the point of view of one of the characters, such as Petra, Calder, or Ms. Hussey?

_____

_____

_____

IV. *Personification*—Personification is a literary device in which an author grants human qualities to nonhuman objects. For example:

The blue shadows of late afternoon were menacing now.

What is being personified?

_____

What mood does this create?

_____

_____

Social Studies Connection:

Do some research to find out about Holland in the seventeenth century when Vermeer was painting his masterpieces. What types of industries and crafts did the Dutch engage in at this time? What guilds existed and how did they function? What was the political and social climate of this time and place? Write a report on your findings and share them with a group of your classmates.

Writing Activities:

1. Write about a time when you or someone you know had to be clever and resourceful in order to solve a mystery. Describe the situation and how you used particular clues to solve the puzzle.

2. Respond to the new letter that the art thief wrote to the newspaper. You may respond as Calder, Petra, or yourself.

CHAPTERS 21 – 24

Vocabulary: Use the context to determine the meaning of the underlined word in each of the following sentences. Then compare your definition to a dictionary definition.

1. All morning Janet <u>stifled</u> her coughs and sneezes, afraid her mother would think she was too ill to go to the party.

   Your definition_____

   Dictionary definition _____

2. Our neighbor was so <u>reclusive</u> that few people on the block could remember ever seeing him.

   Your definition_____

   Dictionary definition _____

3. As long as her children were nearby, the young mother was too <u>preoccupied</u> to carry on a conversation.

   Your definition_____

   Dictionary definition _____

4. In medieval England thieves were common along lonely country roads causing travellers to <u>conceal</u> money in a special pocket.

   Your definition_____

   Dictionary definition _____

5. If you practice every day, you can be <u>confident</u> that you will sing well at the assembly next week.

   Your definition_____

   Dictionary definition _____

6. We could tell from our mother's <u>sober</u> expression that she had some unpleasant news for us.

   Your definition_____

   Dictionary definition _____

7. The crowd gasped while the trapeze artist hung <u>precariously</u> from the single ring, with no safety net below.

   Your definition_____

   Dictionary definition _____

Chapters 21 – 24 (cont.)

> Read to find out whether *A Lady Writing* was rescued.

Questions:

1. Why did Calder and Petra call Mrs. Sharpe at the hospital? How did she respond to them?

2. Why did Calder and Petra enter Delia Dell Hall through the basement entrance?

3. Why was Petra suspicious of her own father's presence in Delia Dell Hall?

4. Why was the number twelve significant to Calder and Petra?

5. Why did Calder steal a "Danger" sign? Was this a successful strategy?

6. Why didn't the policeman believe Petra when she said that the man who assaulted Calder was in possession of the stolen Vermeer painting?

7. Why had Xavier Glitts, also known as Fred Steadman, pretended to be an art scholar and gone to so much trouble to get his hands on the Vermeer painting?

8. What did Petra and Calder learn about the three people they believed to be most involved in the disappearance of *A Lady Writing*?

9. Why wasn't Glitts ever arrested and brought to trial for the theft of the painting?

10. What did Mrs. Sharpe and the children believe after putting together all of the patterns based on the number twelve?

11. How did Petra and Calder's everyday lives change as a result of chasing Vermeer?

Questions for Discussion:

1. Why do you think it is important to preserve the world's art treasures?

2. What parts of this story do you think were realistic? What parts seemed like fantasy?

3. Do you think your own world may consist of unusual relationships and coincidences just waiting to be discovered?

Chapters 21 – 24 (cont.)

Literary Device: Metaphor

What is being compared in the following metaphor?

> Petra and Calder felt separated from everyday life by a chasm of responsibility.

_____

How does the writer's use of figurative language help you to understand the children's feelings?

_____

_____

Literary Element: Setting

The setting of a novel refers to the time and place in which the events of a story occur. How did the setting of Delia Dell Hall contribute to the suspenseful mood of these chapters?

_____

_____

_____

Writing Activities:

1. Write about a time when your first impressions of a person turned out to be wrong. Describe your first impressions and then tell what happened to make you realize that these impressions were inaccurate.

2. Imagine that you are Petra or Calder and write the dialogue for an interview that you have given to a reporter in which you explain how you managed to solve the mystery of the missing painting. Work with a partner to record the interview and then share it with your class.

CLOZE ACTIVITY

The following passage has been taken from Chapter Seven. Read it through completely. Then fill in each blank with a word that makes sense. Afterwards, you may compare your language with that of the author.

Calder flipped back and forth in the book, looking at some of the other

Vermeer paintings. Most of them showed _____ [1] in front of a window;

the Geographer's _____ [2] appeared in many of the paintings, and

_____ [3] same yellow jacket turned up in a _____ [4] of places.

The pictures made you feel _____ [5] though you were peeking in at someone

_____ [6] private moment. The light that came from _____ [7]

made ordinary objects seem important: a quill _____, [8] a pitcher with milk,

an earring, the _____ [9] buttons that were part of a straight-backed

_____. [10] It occurred to Calder that there could _____ [11] hidden

information here — after all, codes involved _____, [12] and the same objects

appeared again and _____ [13] in Vermeer's work. There was the obvious

_____ [14] of windowpanes and floor tiles, and then _____ [15] the

pearls, baskets, pitchers, and framed maps. _____ [16] was symmetry, both

complete and carefully broken.

_____ [17] read more. The book said that Vermeer _____ [18]

penniless when he was in his forties, _____ [19] that almost nothing was

known about his _____. [20] No one understood why such a fabulous

_____ [21] had made only thirty-five works of art. _____ [22] one

knew who the people he painted _____, [23] or why he painted the things he

_____. [24] No one knew how he became an _____. [25]

Vermeer had left behind more questions than answers.

POST-READING ACTIVITIES

1. Return to the K-W-L chart on Vermeer and the Delft School of painting that you began on page four of this study guide. Fill in column three, recording what you learned. Compare your responses to those of your classmates.

2. Return to the Venn diagram to compare the characters of Calder and Petra that you began on page seven of this study guide. Add more information. Compare your responses to those of your classmates.

3. Return to the chart listing the mysteries and their resolutions on page fourteen of this study guide. Fill in the second column. Were any mysteries left unresolved? Do you question any of the resolutions?

4. **Literary Element: Theme**—The theme of a work of fiction refers to the author's message or the central ideas of the work. What are some important themes of *Chasing Vermeer*? List some of the author's ideas about creativity, curiosity, integrity, courage, and friendship.

5. **Art Connection:** Choose another important artist of the seventeenth century and do some research about the artist's life and work. Find some illustrations of this artist's work. Compare this artist's life and work to that of Vermeer.

6. **Readers Theatre:** Choose a chapter or scene within a chapter that has a lot of dialogue (e.g. the tea party at Mrs. Sharpe's house in Chapter Twelve). Each character's dialogue should be read by a different person as though it were a part in a play. One student can be the narrator, reading the descriptive passages. You may wish to use simple props, such as hats or eyeglass frames, when you present your scene to the class.

7. **Literature Circle:** Have a literature circle discussion in which you tell your personal reactions to *Chasing Vermeer*. Here are some questions and sentence starters to help your literature circle begin a discussion:

   - Which character in the novel is most like you? Why?
   - Which elements of the novel seem realistic? Which were added to make the plot more exciting?
   - Did you guess how the author would tie up all the loose threads of the plot? How accurate were your guesses about the novel's climax and conclusion?
   - To whom would you recommend this novel? Why?
   - It was interesting when. . .
   - It was exciting when. . .
   - I wonder. . .
   - Petra learned that. . .
   - Calder learned that. . .

SUGGESTIONS FOR FURTHER READING

* Babbitt, Natalie. *Tuck Everlasting*. Farrar, Straus and Giroux.
* Banks, Lynn Reid. *The Indian in the Cupboard*. Yearling.
* Colfer, Eoin. *Artemis Fowl*. Hyperion.
* Dahl, Roald. *Charlie and the Chocolate Factory*. Penguin.
  Eager, Edward. *Half Magic*. Sandpiper.
* Fitzhugh, Louise. *Harriet the Spy*. Random House.
  Geller, Mark. *What I Heard*. HarperCollins.
* Konigsburg E.L. *From the Mixed-up Files of Mrs. Basil E. Frankweiler*. Athenuem.
  _____. *Up From Jericho Tell*. Athenuem.
* _____. *The View from Saturday*. Aladdin Paperbacks.
* Juster, Norton. *The Phantom Tollbooth*. Yearling.
  L'Engle, Madeleine. *Dragons in the Waters*. Square Fish.
* Paterson, Katherine. *The Great Gilly Hopkins*. HarperCollins.
* Raskin, Ellen. *The Westing Game*. Penguin Putnam.
* Sachar, Louis. *Holes*. Yearling.
* Snyder, Zilpha Keatley. *The Egypt Game*. Athenuem.
* Rowling, J.K. *Harry Potter and the Chamber of Secrets*. Scholastic.
* Snicket, Lemony. *The Bad Beginning* (Book One of A Series of Unfortunate Events.) HarperCollins.
  Yep, Laurence. *The Case of Firecrackers*. HarperCollins.

Reading Challenge
Chevalier, Tracy. *Girl with a Pearl Earring*. Penguin.

Nonfiction
Caroll, Colleen. *How Artists See* series. Abbeville Press.
Janson, Anthony F. *History of Art for Young People*. Harry N. Abrams, Inc.

Websites
www.essentialvermeer.com
www.janvermeer.org
www.artcyclopedia.com/artists/vermeer_jan.html

* NOVEL-TIES Study Guides are available for these titles.

ANSWER KEY

Chapters 1 – 4

Vocabulary: 1. c   2. e   3. g   4. a   5. h   6. b   7. d   8.f;   1. gullible   2. artificial   3. brutal   4. amply   5. agitated   6. flattered   7. determined   8. pretentious

Questions: 1. Three people living alone in Chicago had trouble sleeping one night because they each received an anonymous letter informing them that a crime against an artist had been committed in the past, that they would be rewarded for playing their parts in solving the crime, that they had been chosen for their special qualities, and that their lives would be in danger if they told anybody about the letter. 2. The students in Ms. Hussey's class were excited because she adhered to John Dewey's notion that students should select their own curriculum with teacher guidance. They were fascinated by a teacher who had no preconceived curriculum and seemed open-minded to new pathways to learning that presented themselves. 3. After receiving the first assignment to find out about a letter that changed a person's life, Calder interpreted this to mean he could select the pentomino that represented the letter L, the twelfth letter in the alphabet. He also realized that more than one pentomino for the letter L would form a rectangle, the shape of a letter sent by mail. 4. Petra was upset by her encounters with Calder and Ms. Hussey at Powell's Used Books because she was a quiet, introverted person, used to pursuing her interests on her own; the idea of sharing these with others was unpleasant to her, as was the idea that she might be forced to socialize with a classmate and a teacher. 5. Petra was unhappy at home because she would prefer a quiet, orderly place rather than an untidy, raucous environment where she lived with her numerous siblings. 6. The author described both Petra and Calder as "hybrid" kids because they both came from racially and ethnically mixed families. 7. The purpose of the field trip to the Art Institute of Chicago was to find artwork depicting a letter of some significance.

Chapters 5 – 8

Vocabulary: 1. c   2. d   3. a   4. f   5. g   6. b   7. h   8. e;   1. profound   2. inexplicable   3. reproduction   4. bizarre   5. exhilarating   6. venomous   7. disoriented   8. mediocre

Questions: 1. Petra was fascinated by Charles Fort's book because he had gleaned hundreds of stories of unusual sightings which he found in newspapers from around the world. She thought this book would satisfy Ms. Hussey's assignment to describe a piece of art. 2. When Charles Fort wrote, "We fit standards to judgments," he meant that people try to fit all of experience into their own view of the world. They try "to fit everything that happened to them into something they could understand." 3. Petra learned from her vision of the old-fashioned woman who appeared to her in a half-dream that she herself belonged in "a writer's world" where words and images were chosen with care and sensitivity; this vision helped to crystallize Petra's love of language into a desire to be a writer. 4. Calder chose the picture on his cherished wooden box to fulfill Ms. Hussey's art assignment because it was puzzling and gave him a new way of looking at things; thus, satisfying his own definition of art. 5. Calder was interested in Mrs. Sharpe because she had been seen outside his house with Ms. Hussey and Mr. Watch. Petra was interested because she was the recorded former possessor of the book, *Lo!*. 6. Mrs. Sharpe invited Calder and his friend Petra to tea because she wanted to get to know the two young people who were as fascinated with the book *Lo!* as she was. 7. Calder was amazed by the painting that hung on Mrs. Sharpe's wall because it was a copy of Vermeer's painting, *The Geographer*, the same image as the one that appeared on top of his precious box. 8. Calder was intrigued by Jan Vermeer's use of patterns and repeated symbolism in various paintings, as well as by the mysteries that surrounded his relatively brief life and scant but marvelous artistic output. 9. Petra was shocked to see a copy of the painting, *A Lady Writing*, because she had fashioned her Halloween costume after a vision she had in a dream: she didn't realize that she had dreamed of someone who had appeared in an oil painting done in 1665 by Jan Vermeer.

Chapters 9 – 12

Vocabulary: 1. c   2. d   3. h   4. b   5. g   6. a   7. f   8. e;   1. attribute   2. intimidated   3. obscurity   4. instantaneous   5. judicious   6. subdued   7. ingenious   8. incalculable

Questions: 1. Hoping to find out whether there was any connection or guiding principle to explain the many coincidences they were experiencing, Petra and Calder decided to do some research on Vermeer's life. In doing so, they expected to find some pattern in the repeated symbols or the solution to a riddle. 2. Calder and Petra called the National Gallery of Art to find out if the Vermeer painting, *A Lady Writing*, was safe on its walls. They feared that all of the strange coincidences they were experiencing forebode danger for the painting. 3. Calder was worried about his father because he seemed distracted, upset about a letter, and unwilling to share the source of his anxiety with his son. 4. Petra and Calder were particularly upset about the theft of the Vermeer painting, *A Lady*

Writing, because they both had recently become interested in the painting, were intrigued that it should have been selected for an exhibit in Chicago, and its theft confirmed their premonition that the painting was in danger. 5. Calder and Petra were worried about Ms. Hussey because her injured arm suggested to them that she might be in danger from an entity that had something to do with the Vermeer coincidences. 6. The painting was stolen by an art scholar who wanted the public to pressure officials to discover the truth about Vermeer's paintings: were they actually painted by the master at the height of his career or were they painted by an immature Vermeer, or by lesser artists. This person now chose to write an open letter because having committed the art theft, he or she now needed wide support of the project of authenticating some of Vermeer's paintings. 7. The Vermeer case helped to teach Ms. Hussey's students about art scholarship by getting them involved in the process of authenticating paintings and attributing them to the correct source. They studied reproductions to find similarities and differences in the various paintings to see if they all appeared to be executed by the same person. 8. Calder was amazed because entering Mrs. Sharpe's kitchen was like walking into the world of one of Vermeer's paintings. 9. Mrs. Sharpe responded to Petra's and Calder's questions bluntly and enigmatically. Her attitude about the theft and lack of concern for the morality of it suggested that she was at least sympathetic to the art thief, and possibly might have been involved in the scholarly crime.

Chapters 13 – 16
Vocabulary: 1. b 2. d 3. a 4. c 5. b 6. a 7. c 8. d
Questions: 1. Petra and Calder worried that Ms. Hussey might have received one of the three letters and was in danger, or that she had been more directly implicated in the theft itself. 2. The authorities decided not to allow the publication of further messages from the art bandit because these messages were attracting too much publicity; thus rewarding the thief with too much attention. 3. Calder was eager to deliver the books because he wanted to snoop around Mrs. Sharpe's house to determine if she had any part in the art theft. 4. Calder thought he had to rescue Tommy because his coded message reported that his stepfather moved out and he and his Mom were stranded in New York. 5. Calder's father recalled that the late Mr. Sharpe had been a Vermeer scholar who was murdered in an apparently random act of violence many years before. The children doubted the accuracy of his remarks because they immediately suspected a connection between Mr. Sharpe's area of study and his untimely death, and doubted that it was a "random" crime. The information about Vermeer that Mr. Sharpe had been on the verge of announcing suggests that the children were correct to be suspicious about his death. 6. Mrs. Sharpe requested police protection because the letter contained a threat of violence. 7. Ms. Hussey was released from jail quickly because she confessed to the police that she had received a letter identical to the one Mrs. Sharpe had received; this indicated that she was not the criminal, but rather a potential victim who also needed protection. 8. Petra and Calder jumped to the conclusion that Ms. Hussey and Mrs. Sharpe were involved in the theft of the Vermeer painting. They thought that Ms. Hussey might have hidden the painting and Mrs. Sharpe knew where it was. 9. Petra and Calder decided to search the University School premises for the missing canvas because they believed that if Ms. Hussey was involved in the scheme, she would have hidden the painting close by, where no one would suspect its presence.

Chapters 17 – 20
Vocabulary: 1. fraud 2. courtyard 3. vigorously 4. elegant 5. murky 6. luminous 7. brusque 8. geologist
Questions: 1. The Vermeer art theft and its media publicity had the positive effects of making many people, who were otherwise uninterested in art, become amateur art critics, visit museums, and, in general, become comfortable with art. 2. Mrs. Sharpe was taken to the hospital because she slipped and hurt her leg as she was trying to put the letter to Ms. Hussey into the mail. 3. Petra and Calder were spared the illegal act of opening Mrs. Sharpe's letter to Ms. Hussey, and thus avoided the possible path to "a life of crime" when someone scooped up the letter that had dropped to the ground and mailed it. 4. Mrs. Sharpe forgave the children after Petra confessed that they had almost opened her letter to Ms. Hussey because they reminded her of herself—bright, inquisitive, and adventurous. She also reminded the children that Charles Fort would have approved of their desire to find the truth, even if she did not approve of them reading anyone's mail. 5. Tommy added more mystery when he informed Calder that he received a postcard from the missing boy called "Frog," and that one side of it had a reproduction of a Vermeer painting from the National Gallery. 6. Mrs. Sharpe seemed to give the children clues to the whereabouts of the missing painting when she arranged the pentimenoes on her hospital bed and suggested particular words that could be made from them; the words possibly formed a coded message that the painting had been hidden in Delia Dell Hall. 7. Petra's father called the scholarly terrorist a "lunatic" because this person had written an open letter threatening to

destroy *A Lady Writing* if the attributions of the questionable Vermeer paintings were not changed within a month. 8. The art thief believed the demands would be met by art historians and museum curators because they supported the new point of view about the authenticity of certain paintings usually attributed to Vermeer. Since newspapers and an author had shown sympathy for this point of view, the art thief felt the time was ripe to press the point home through the threat of destroying the painting.

Chapters 21 – 24

Vocabulary: 1. stifled—smothered; cut off   2. reclusive—solitary; prone to shutting oneself away 3. preoccupied—lost in thought; already occupied   4. conceal—hide   5. confident—certain 6. sober—very serious; subdued   7. precariously—dangerously; uncertainly

Questions: 1. Calder and Petra called Mrs. Sharpe because they thought she might have had something to do with the last public letter and that she could tell them where to search in Delia Dell Hall. Mrs. Sharpe's response to the children was cold and abrupt. She warned them to beware of danger. 2. Calder and Petra entered Delia Dell Hall through a basement entrance because a man with a European accent, perhaps the same man they encountered at the post office, took notice of them at the front entrance and acknowledged that he had seen them at the hall the day before. 3. Petra was suspicious of her father's presence in Delia Dell Hall because he did not normally work on this side of the campus; he had been carrying a package the approximate size of the missing canvas, but when joined by the strange man, he was no longer carrying the package; and Petra had heard her father make many cryptic remarks recently concerning the art theft. 4. The number twelve was significant to Calder and Petra because they both had the same birthday— 12/12; there were twelve pentominoes; there were twelve wood panels on the staircase, and behind one they found the painting; the lady in the painting had twelve pearls. At the end of the story, Calder discovered that all of the characters had twelve-letter names. 5. Calder stole a "Danger" sign in order to wrap it up to appear as though it might be the stolen Vermeer painting. This way, if he and Petra were pursued, Calder could deflect all the attention, allowing Petra to escape with the painting. The strategy allowed Petra to escape with the painting from the man they saw in Delia Dell Hall. 6. The policemen didn't believe Petra when she said that the man who assaulted Calder was in possession of the stolen Vermeer painting because he assumed that she was making up a story, trying to capitalize on the famous case that had the whole world talking. 7. Xavier Glitts had gone to so much trouble to get his hands on the Vermeer painting because a wealthy client had promised him sixty million dollars if he could steal the painting; he posed as a scholarly thief because he wanted to draw the attention of the authorities away from the simply mercenary motives of art thieves. He hoped that this ruse would allow him to get away with the theft and sale of the painting. 8. Petra and Calder learned that all three of these people who had received the letters and might have been involved in the disappearance of the painting were actually innocent of wrong-doing and intrigue, and shared a knowledge of and passion for art. 9. Glitts was never arrested and brought to trial for the theft of the painting because he died of a heart attack on the train while escaping from the authorities. 10. After putting together all of the patterns based on the number twelve, Mrs. Sharpe and the children believed that anything was possible, and that events attributed to chance might in fact have a mysterious and meaningful connection. 11. As a result of chasing Vermeer, the lives of Petra and Calder became rich in relationships with others, such as Ms. Hussey and Mrs. Sharpe. They also had become good friends who would continue to discuss the fantastic possibilities of the world around them.

NOTES: